HAPPY TIME DESIGNS

40 Hand Drawn Designs to Color

I0420094

By
Sherry Watkins

Edited by Angel Thornhill

https://www.facebook.com/happytimedesigns/

https://www.facebook.com/happytimedesigns/
ISBN : 9781518617751

COLORING TIPS

This book is best with color pencils, gel pens, or markers. Wet mediums should be used sparingly. While the illustrations are single sided to help prevent bleed through to the next picture, I suggest placing several sheets of paper, or a sheet of card stock, behind the page that you are working on just in case the markers bleed through.

Cover Design by Shelah Dow

Cover Art Colorists

Patricia Burke - #19
Dereseé Cundiff - #40
T-Robyn Lyle - #33
Deirdre Gamill-Hock - #18

You're all so talented and I thank you so very much for helping us make this beautiful cover!

Finally, Thank YOU for trying out my book! I look forward to seeing your finished pages! Feel free to share them with me at https://www.facebook.com/happytimedesigns/. I hope you like my designs, and enjoy making them your own with your own unique style as you bring them to life.

Special Thanks

Special thanks to my daughter, Angel. When the idea of a coloring book came about from all my drawings piling up, you volunteered your time make it happen. You edited all of the pages, got them formatted, and overall handled all the little details to help me get this thing published. Thank you so much!! I appreciate all your hard work that went into making this happen! Another special thanks to Shelah Dow. Your experience and consultations were crucial to publishing this book. We kept hitting devastating roadblocks due to a fundamental lack of knowledge for a project like this and you saved us. Also, the cover you designed for us is amazing! We couldn't possibly thank you enough Shelah! Shelah is a wonderful artist herself, check out her work @ ShelahDowArt.com

This book is dedicated to Noelle Rose Watkins

The creation of many of these designs happened after we lost you sweet girl. My heart heavy with loss and grief, I spent day after day drawing to memories of your joyful smile and big blue eyes. You were the best mix of a happy sweet girl and a hilarious amount of sassiness. I would like to think that these designs capture a bit of your fun-loving spirit. Though you were with us only briefly, you had a deep impact on everyone who knew you and you will never be forgotten. My little NoellyBelly, you will be forever cherished in our hearts.

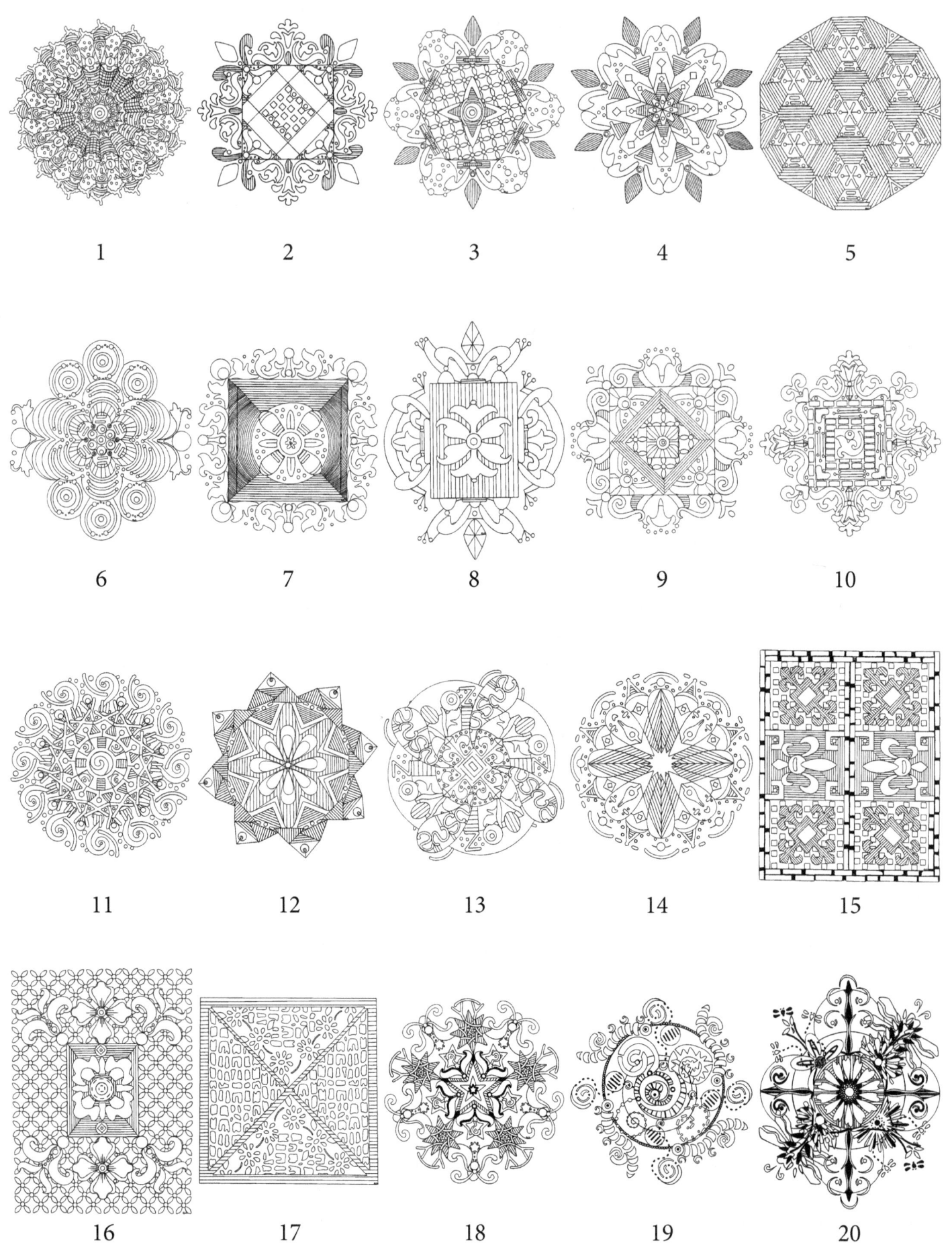

1   2   3   4   5

6   7   8   9   10

11   12   13   14   15

16   17   18   19   20

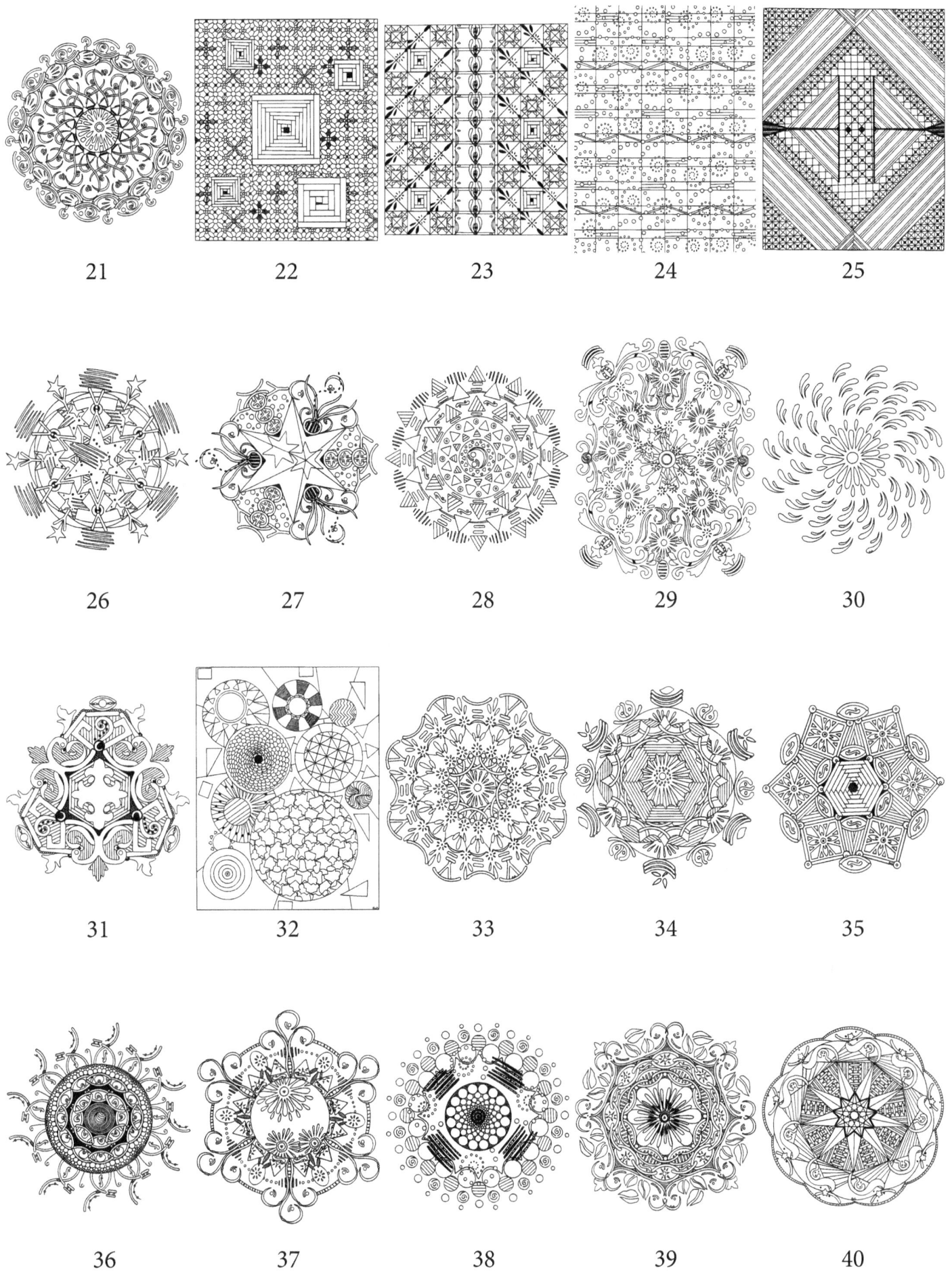

21 22 23 24 25

26 27 28 29 30

31 32 33 34 35

36 37 38 39 40

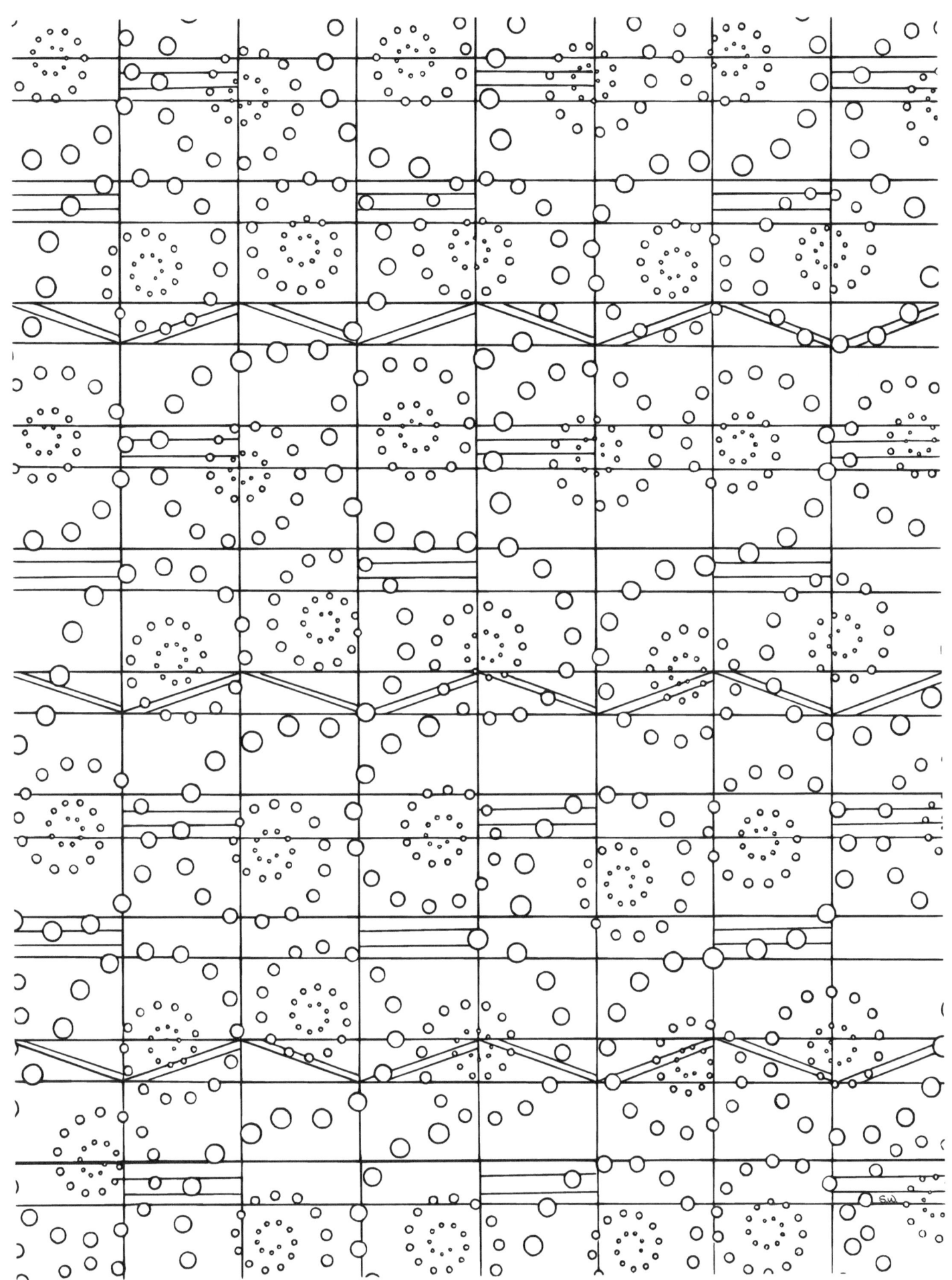

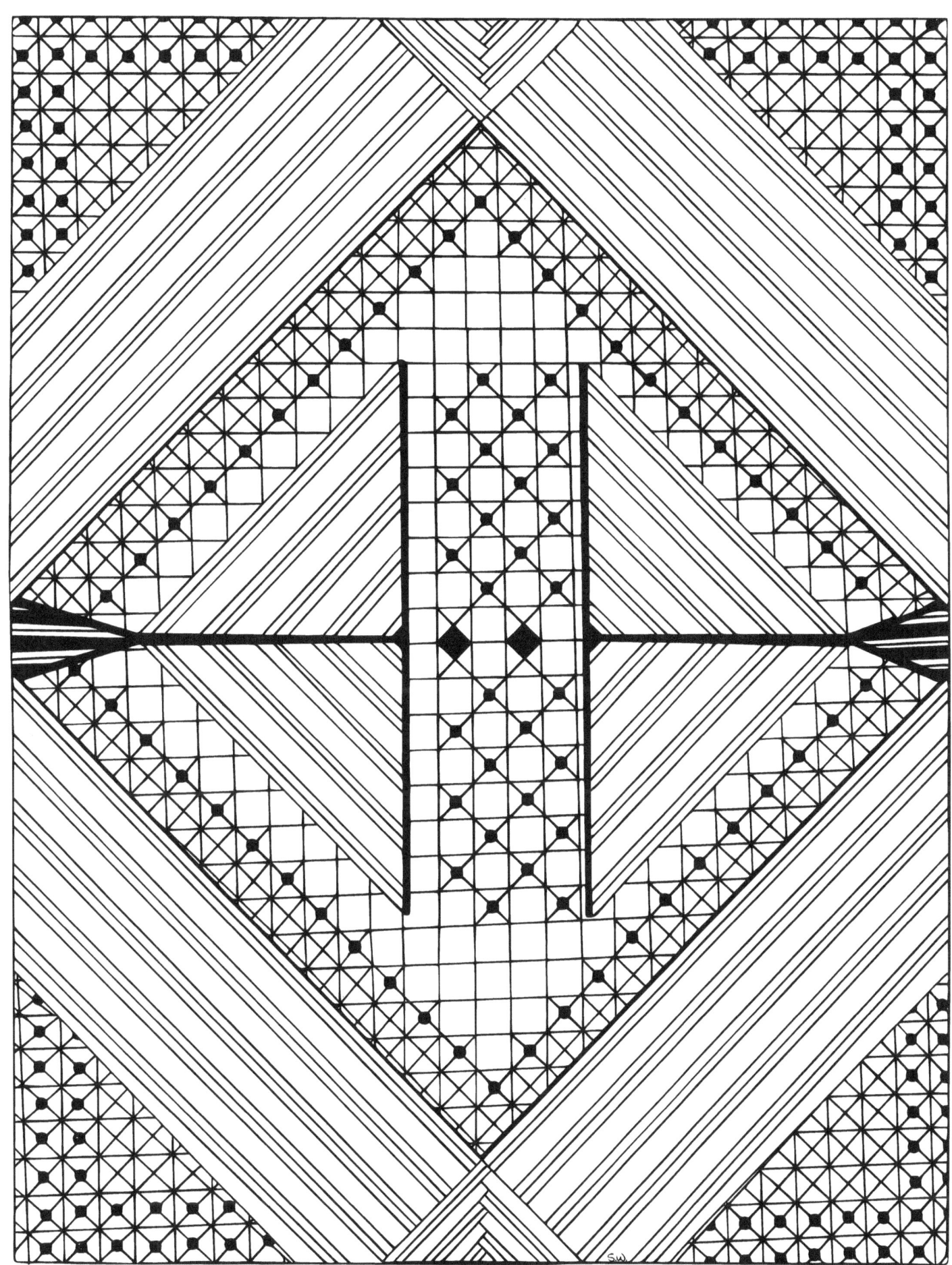

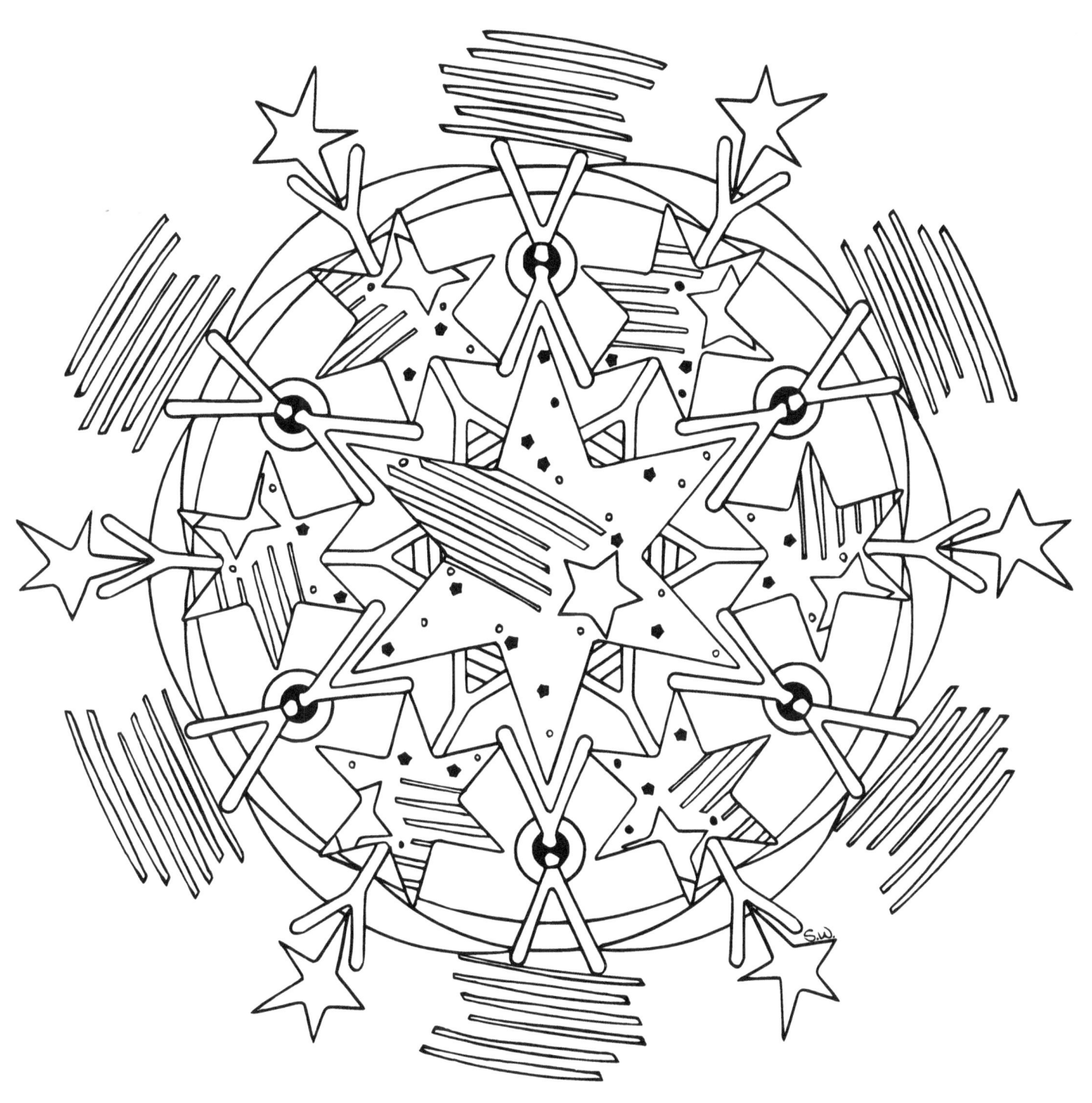

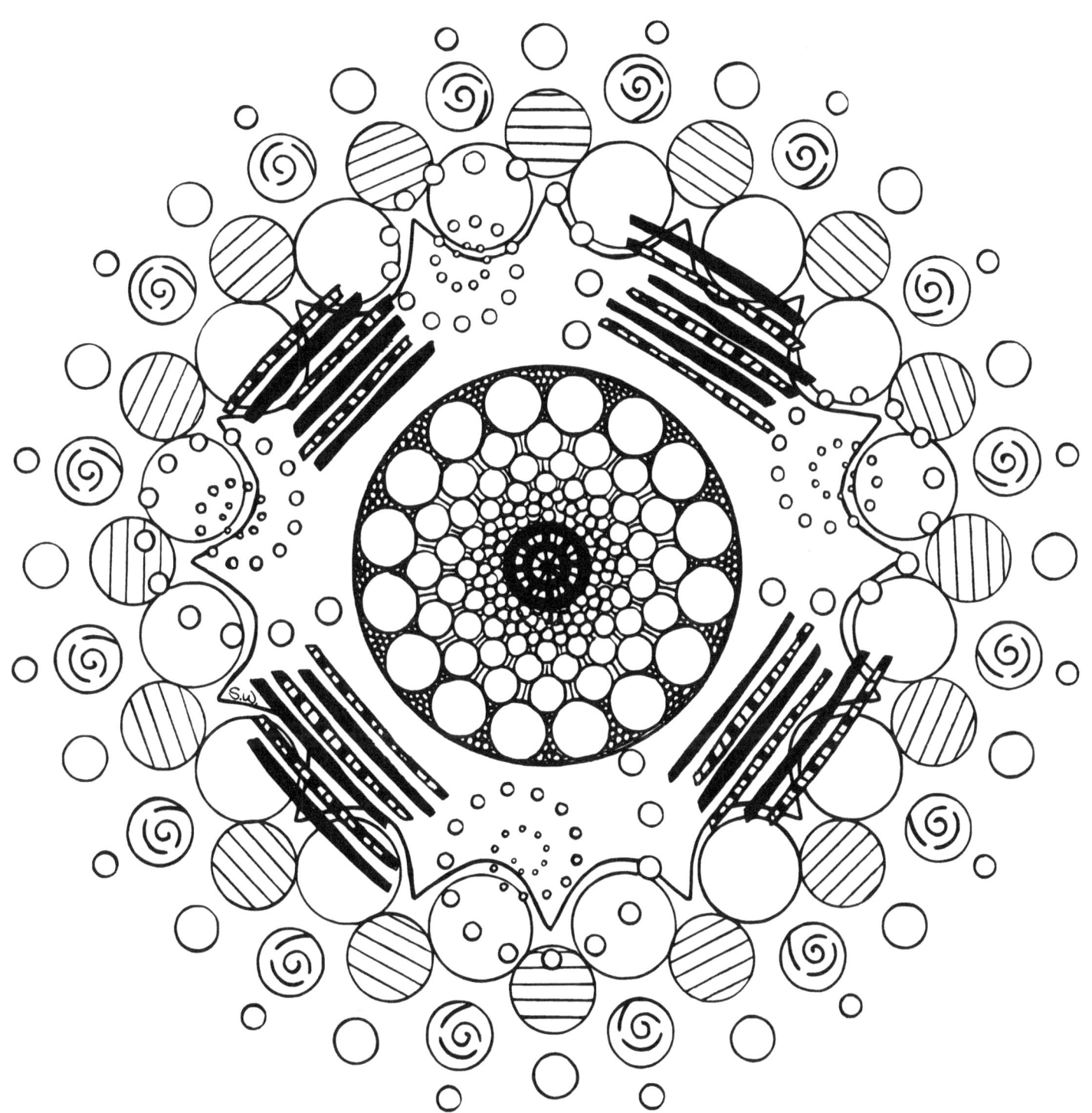

THIS IS THE END OF THE BOOK, THE FOLLOWING
PAGES ARE PROVIDED FOR COLOR AND BLENDING
TESTING

THANK YOU!

© Sherry Watkins 2018 - Happy Time Designs - Color Testing Page 1

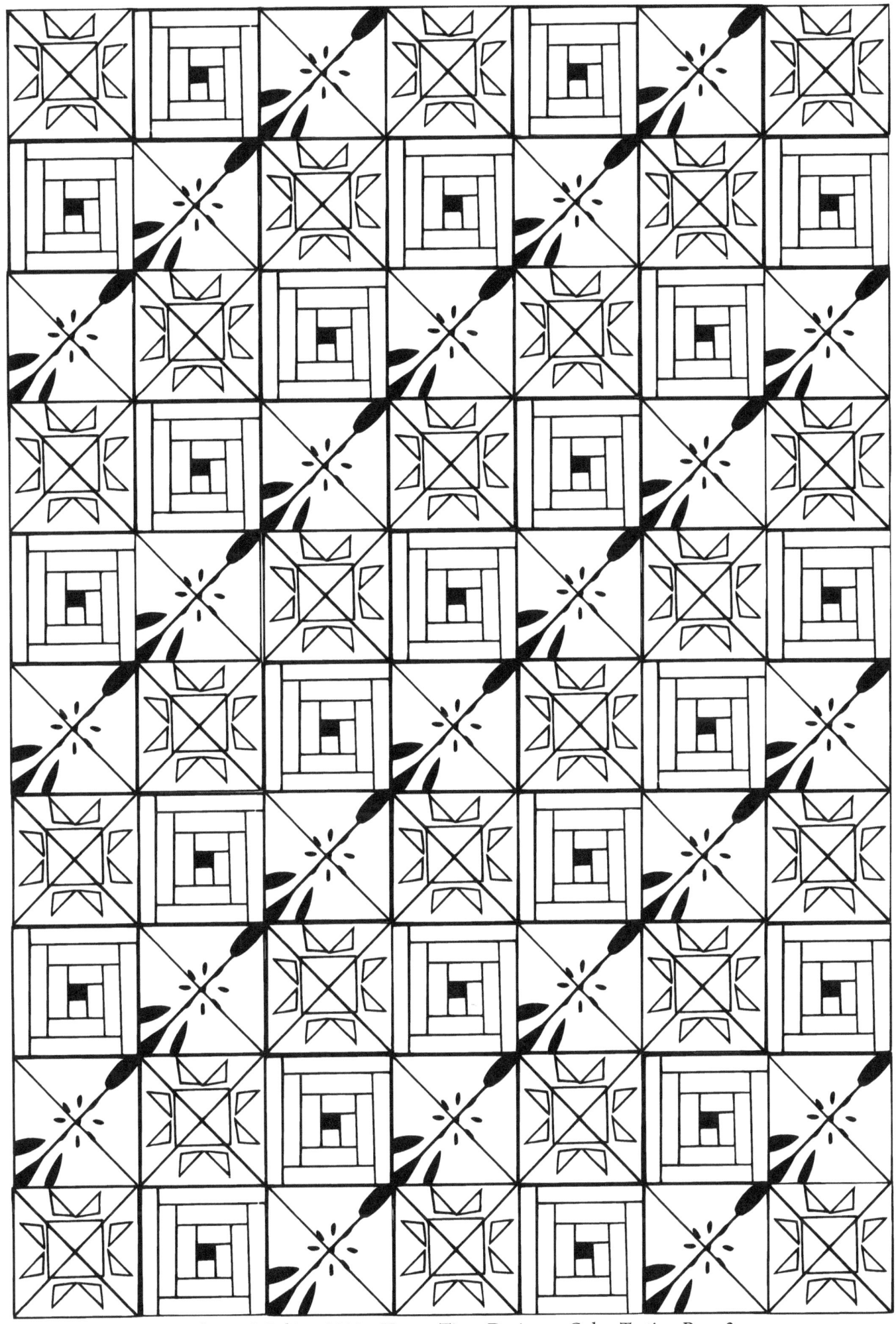

This Page Intentionally Left Blank

This Page Intentionally Left Blank